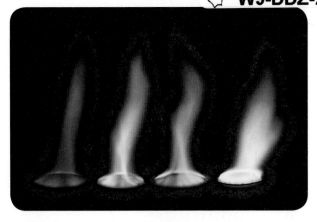

Are You a Scientist?

by Susan Jones Leeming

PEARSON

Glenview, Illinois
Boston, Massachusetts
Chandler, Arizona
Upper Saddle River, New Jersey

Photographs
Every effort has been made to secure permission and provide appropriate credit for photographic material.
The publisher deeply regrets any omission and pledges to correct errors called to its attention in subsequent editions.

Unless otherwise acknowledged, all photographs are the copyright © of Dorling Kindersley, a division of Pearson.

Photo locators denoted as follows: Top (T), Center (C), Bottom (B), Left (L), Right (R), Background (Bkgd)

Opener: (C) Jim Cummins/Corbis; FP5 (C) Jim Cummins/Corbis; Tek Image/Photo Researchers, Inc.; 3 ©Will & Deni McIntyre/Photo Researchers, Inc.; 4 ©Steve Chenn/Corbis; 5 ©Roger Ressmeyer/Corbis; 8 Tek Image/Photo Researchers, Inc.; 10 ©Roger Ressmeyer/Corbis; 11 ©Annie Griffiths Belt/Corbis; 19 British Antarctic Survey /Photo Researchers, Inc.; 22 ©Jim Cummins/Corbis; 23 NASA.

ISBN-13: 978-0-328-61784-5
ISBN-10:   0-328-61784-9

5 6 7 8 9 10 V0FL 16 15 14 13

Scientists help us understand how the world works. As people understand more, they use knowledge to improve the way things are done.

Tools help people do work more easily. A tool can be as simple as a hammer, or as complex as a computer. Using knowledge to design new tools and new ways of doing things is called technology.

Technology is at work all around you. Your home is full of technology. The plumbing system and electrical system are technologies that work together so you can take a hot shower.

Hammers are tools.

An invention is something made for the first time. One important invention is the computer. A computer is a machine that stores, processes, and sends electronic information quickly. There are computer chips in ovens, clocks, cars, phones, airplanes, and trains.

In this book you will learn how scientists from each area of science help us understand more about our world.

Computers help scientists in many different ways.

What is a scientist?

Scientists are men and women who study the universe and how it works. There is a lot to study in our huge universe. Scientists often make new discoveries that affect our lives. Scientific discoveries can help treat diseases, predict natural disasters, explore other planets and stars, and even find new species of animals.

Some scientific work is done in laboratories.

Scientists can learn a lot about how Earth works by conducting experiments outside.

Since the universe is so big, science has been divided into different areas. The different areas are physical and chemical science, life science, and Earth and space science. Physicists, chemists, biologists, Earth scientists, and astronomers each study something different about the universe.

Many scientists often study just one thing. A biologist may spend a lifetime studying one ant species. A physicist may study just one group of stars. But all scientists observe, hypothesize, test, and analyze. These are the steps that scientists follow to test their ideas about how the universe works.

Testing Ideas

When scientists want to learn more about something, they start by observing it. To observe something means to examine or study it closely. As scientists observe, they often come up with an idea to explain what they see. This idea is called a hypothesis. Once scientists have come up with a hypothesis, they must test it to see if it can be supported. Scientists conduct experiments to test their hypotheses.

Observation is very important when testing new scientific ideas.

Here, a flame is being observed. The hypothesis is that the flame needs oxygen to burn. The flame goes out when the oxygen is gone. The hypothesis receives support!

Experiments are usually carried out in laboratories. Laboratories are clean places where scientists can repeat the same experiment many times. Scientists are able to control many factors in laboratories, such as temperature and time.

Sometimes the results of repeated experiments support the hypothesis. Other times they do not. If they do, the scientists can develop a theory to share with others. A theory is an explanation based on observation and experiments. If the results do not support the hypothesis, the scientists must develop and test a new one.

Analyzing Results

Scientists use tools to gather data in the form of measurements. Careful measurements are very important in scientific experiments. If measurements are not exact the results might not be correct. Then they use graphs, mathematics, and computers to analyze their results. To analyze something means to examine it carefully and draw a conclusion. After scientists analyze their results, they know if their hypothesis was supported.

Analyzing DNA results can give scientists a lot of information.

Some scientists study how diseases can pass from parents to their children. These scientists observe genetic material called deoxyribonucleic acid (DNA). DNA is passed from parents to children. Scientists often come up with a hypothesis about how

Tools, such as this scale, help scientists gather exact data.

a disease could be passed on in DNA. Next they test their hypothesis by studying the DNA of thousands of people with and without that disease.

The results of their studies must be analyzed. Scientists who study how diseases are inherited may make graphs of healthy and sick people to try to understand their results better. If the results of their studies support their hypothesis, the scientists may develop a theory. Then the theory can be shared with others.

Fieldwork

Not all observation takes place in laboratories. Sometimes scientists must go outdoors to observe what they are studying. This is known as fieldwork. Fieldwork may take a scientist to the side of a volcano to investigate the possibility of an eruption occurring. It could also take a scientist to the bank of a river to observe and test the river's water.

Volcanologists must do a lot of their work outside, often in dangerous conditions.

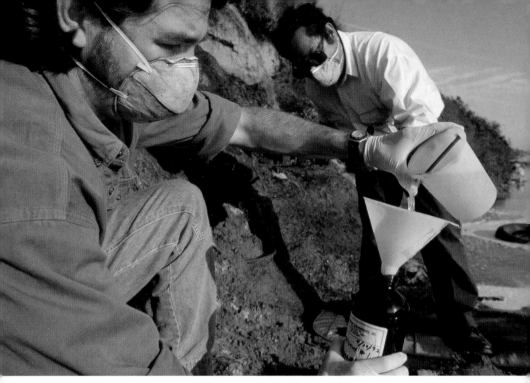

These scientists are checking for pollution in river water.

In addition to observation, these scientists might also conduct outdoor experiments to test their hypotheses. In a laboratory, scientists are able to control many factors. But wind, water, and sunlight can damage or affect an experiment done outside. It is much more difficult to analyze fieldwork results. Scientists usually need to conduct many experiments to be certain of their results. Yet fieldwork is still an important part of scientific research. Sometimes it is the only way scientists can learn when a volcano may erupt or whether river water is safe to drink.

Physicists

Physics is the area of science that studies energy, matter, and motion. Almost everything in the universe is made up of matter. Physicists try to understand the basic laws that explain the whole universe. Because physics is such a big area of study, most physicists concentrate on one small part. Some physicists study motion and how matter moves. Other physicists might help airplane engineers in designing faster, lighter airplanes.

Some physicists study forces and motion.

Astrophysicists study space and the objects in it.

Atomic or nuclear physicists study matter. They search for the basic particles that make up everything. They study some of the smallest particles in the universe, such as atoms. Nuclear energy, a powerful energy source, was discovered by nuclear physicists.

Astrophysicists study objects in space. Astrophysicists work with astronomers or space scientists to explain how matter and energy behave in space. Many principles of physics are used to explain ideas in all the other areas of science.

Chemists

Chemistry is the part of science that studies elements. Elements are the basic substances that all materials are made of. There are more than one hundred elements in the universe. Chemists investigate how elements behave. They conduct lots of experiments to do this. They also study chemical reactions. This is when substances mix, break down, and form new substances.

If potassium iodide and lead nitrate solutions are mixed together, they form solid lead iodide.

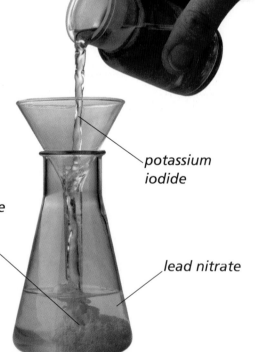

potassium iodide

solid lead iodide forms when solutions react

lead nitrate

Like physicists, chemists often focus on one area of study. Some chemists study a single element. Organic chemists only study substances that contain the element carbon.

Other chemists may work on creating new substances, such as plastic or nylon. Chemists also try to improve substances. They may conduct experiments to try to discover ways to make a substance stronger or lighter.

Chemists can use flame tests to identify the elements in some chemicals.

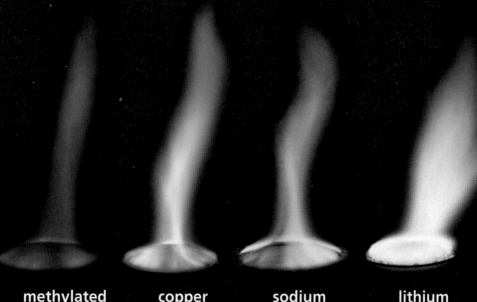

| methylated spirit | copper salts | sodium salts | lithium salts |

Biologists

Biology is the study of organisms or living things. Biologists examine the structure, or makeup, of living things. They also study what goes on inside organisms and the environments where organisms live. Plants and animals are both organisms. One way to split biology is into the fields of botany and zoology. Botanists study plants and zoologists study animals. Within these fields, most biologists study a specific organism or group of organisms.

Some botanists may spend a lifetime studying cacti.

Biologists classify organisms into different animal groups.

There are many more than the two million known types of living things on Earth. Biologists classify, or separate, all these different organisms into groups. They give each one a scientific name. This makes it easier for biologists to recognize the similarities and differences between living things.

Sometimes biology is combined with other sciences. This can be helpful if a biologist wants to study one part of an organism. Biochemists study chemistry and how it relates to organisms. Biologists also work with people who teach others how to protect and conserve the environment and the organisms that live in it.

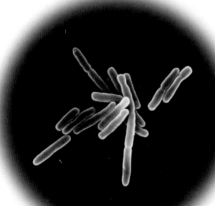

One group of organisms that biologists study is bacteria.

Earth Scientists

Earth scientists explain our physical world to us. They study the physical characteristics of Earth. These scientists study volcanoes, tides, and fossils. They even study hurricanes and the reasons why the landscape looks the way it does today. Like physics, Earth science is a big area of science. Many Earth scientists use physics, chemistry, and biology to help them study our planet. There are several different areas within Earth science.

Some Earth scientists study fossils.

Grand Canyon

Geologists are Earth scientists who examine Earth's history. They look at the substances that make up Earth and how they are arranged. Some geologists study huge landscapes such as the Grand Canyon. Other geologists examine prehistoric fossils or rock formations.

Meteorologists focus on the atmosphere. These scientists observe, record, and try to predict the weather.

Oceanographers study the oceans and the ocean floor. They explore and experiment with tides, underwater volcanoes, and the effects of ocean patterns on the land.

Weather balloons can measure temperature, humidity, and air pressure.

Applying Science

Technology changes people's lives in amazing ways. Biologists who study botany may discover a better way to grow plants. Technology puts this discovery to work in farm fields, so we can grow more food. Chemists may discover a new substance that can fight a disease. Technology puts this substance to work in vaccines, so we can live long, healthy lives. Meteorologists may discover an area where strong winds always blow. Technology puts this knowledge to work when wind farms are built to produce electricity we can use.

wind farm

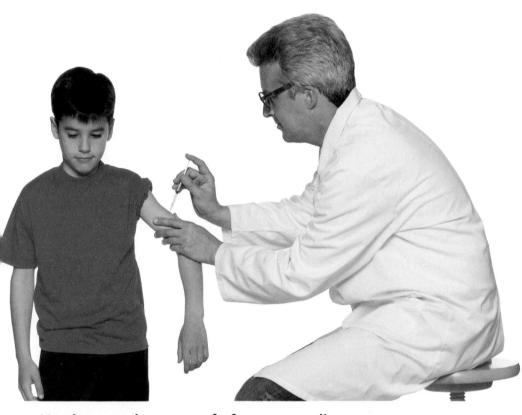

Vaccines can keep us safe from many diseases.

Scientists observe our world, make hypotheses about it, test those hypotheses, and publish theories when their hypotheses are supported.

Many other people use scientific discoveries in their work. Other scientists, engineers, and doctors use scientific theories in their own work. The different areas of science benefit everyone in many ways. Science is applied in our world every day.

A Voyage of Discovery

Could you be a scientist? School science classes could help you to become a geologist. Then you could observe and analyze fossils or rocks. Or you could become an astrophysicist. Then you could study space and the beginnings of the universe. Maybe you find biology more interesting. You could discover new species or help save ones in danger of becoming extinct.

Study science in your classroom!

What will scientists of the future be looking for?

Science is the study of the universe and everything in it. The possibilities for discovery are never ending. Just look around you. The plants, animals, people, rocks, water, and sky are all waiting to be observed, tested, and analyzed. You can make a difference in the world using science. Your voyage of discovery in science is waiting to begin.

Glossary

analyze to examine carefully and draw a conclusion

botany science of plants

hypothesis an explanation of an observation that must be tested

laws theories about the universe that always receive support and cannot easily be changed

nuclear related to the nucleus or center of an atom; nuclear energy is produced when atoms are either split or combined

theory an explanation based on observation and experiments

zoology science of animals